Safe with God

BIBLE CHAPTERS
FOR KIDS

When I stay close
to the Lord, I can rest
and be at peace.

"He that dwells in the
secret place of the most
High will abide under the
shadow of the Almighty."

(verse 1)

I know that I can trust
the Lord, because
He protects me and
makes me strong.

"I will say of the Lord, He is
my refuge and my fortress: my
God; in Him will I trust."

(verse 2)

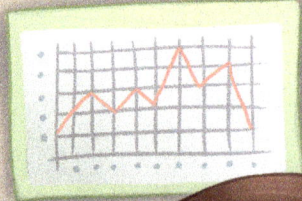

The Lord can protect
me from those who want
to hurt me, and can
keep me healthy.

"Surely He will deliver you
from the snare of the fowler, and
from the deadly pestilence."

(verse 3)

The Lord covers me, like a bird covers its baby. He guards me faithfully.

"He will cover you with his feathers, and under his wings will you trust: His truth will be your shield and buckler."

(verse 4)

I don't have to be afraid of the dark, nor of anything during the day.

"You will not be afraid
for the terror by night;
nor for the arrow that
flies by day;"

(verse 5)

I don't have
to fear sickness,
because the Lord
is with me.

"Nor for the pestilence that walks
in darkness; nor for the destruction
that strikes at midday."

(verse 6)

Even if there is war
or chaos all around
me, I can feel safe
with the Lord.

"A thousand will fall at your
side, and ten thousand at
your right hand; but it will not
come near you."

(verse 7)

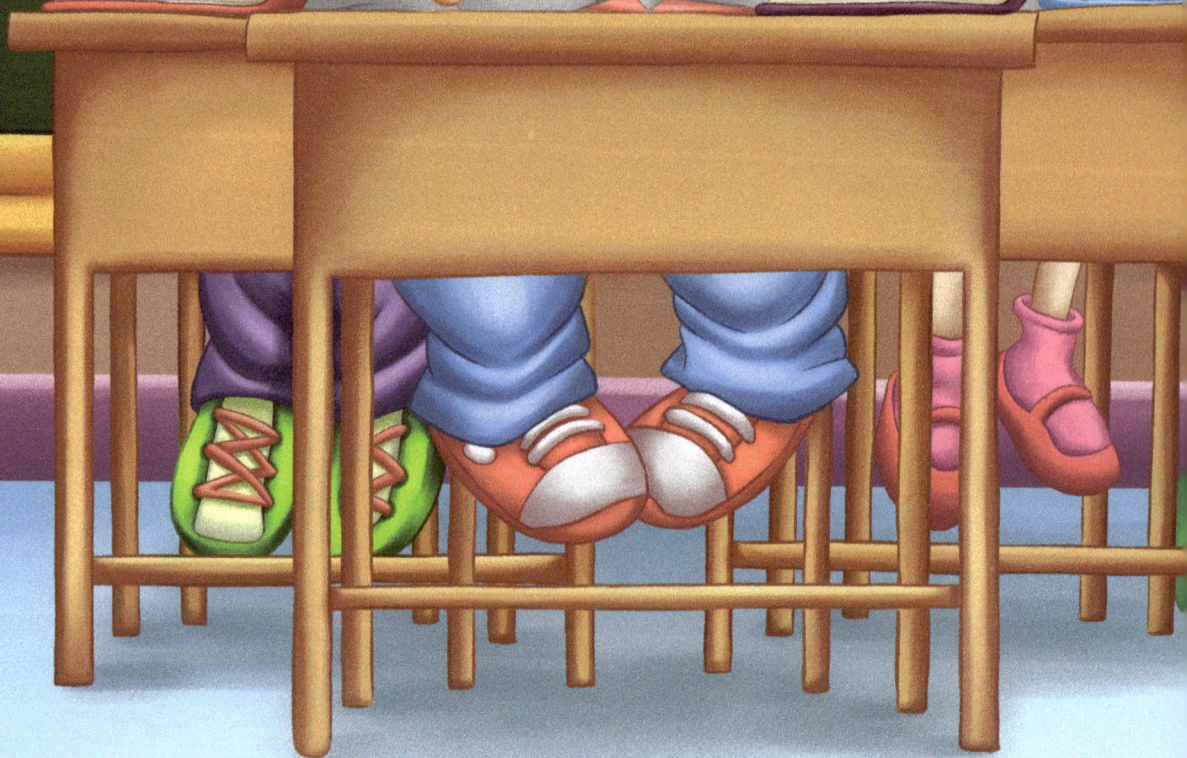

I see what happens to those who do wrong things, so I don't want to copy them.

"Only with your eyes will you behold and see the reward of the wicked."

(verse 8)

The Lord protects
me like a fortress, so
when I am with Him,
nothing can harm me.

"Because you have made the Lord,
which is my refuge, even the most
High, your habitation; There will no
evil befall you, now will any plague
come near your dwelling."

(verse 9,10)

The Lord tells His
angels to be my body
guards wherever I go.

"For He will give His angels charge over
you, to keep you in all your ways."
(verse 11)

They watch over me,
so I don't get hurt.

"They will hold you up in their hands, lest
you dash your foot against a stone."

(verse 12)

The Lord's angels are strong enough to help me even in dangerous places.

"You will tread on the lion and adder: the young lion and the dragon will you trample under feet." (verse 13)

The Lord loves me,
and I love Him. That's
why He wants to
keep me safe.

"Because he has set his love on Me,
therefore will I deliver him: I will set him on
high, because he has known My name."

(verse 14)

The Lord says that when I pray and call out to Him, that He will come and rescue me.

"He will call on Me, and I will answer him: I will be with him in trouble; I will deliver him, and honour him." (verse 15)

The Lord loves
to care for me so
that I can live a
long and healthy
life with Him.

"With long life will I satisfy him,
and show him My salvation."

(verse 16)

More books in the series:

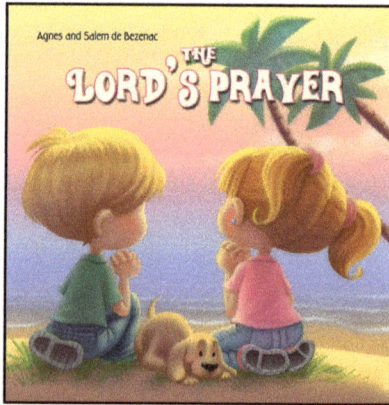

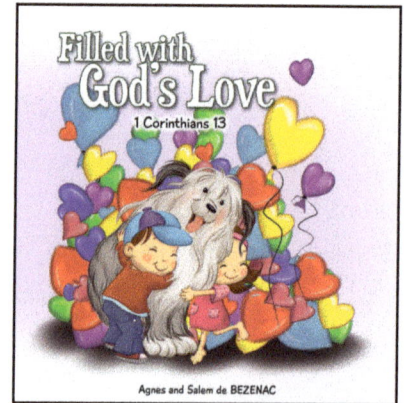

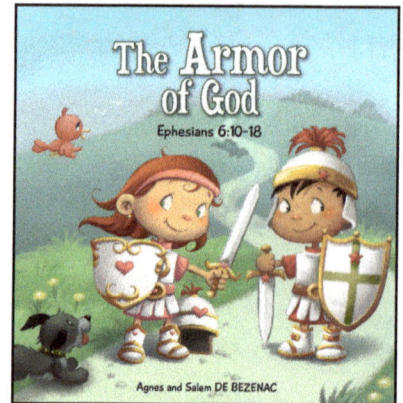

THE LORD'S PRAYER — Agnes and Salem de Bezenac

PSALM 119 — Agnes and Salem

Filled with God's Love — 1 Corinthians 13 — Agnes and Salem de BEZENAC

PROVERBS

My Shepherd — Psalm 23 — Agnes and Salem de BEZENAC

The Armor of God — Ephesians 6:10-18 — Agnes and Salem DE BEZENAC

iCHARACTER

Published by iCharacter Ltd. (Ireland)
www.icharacter.org
By Agnes and Salem de Bezenac
Illustrated by Agnes de Bezenac
Colored by Henny Y.
Copyright. All rights reserved.
All Bible verses adapted from the KJV.

www.ingramcontent.com/pod-product-compliance
Lightning Source LLC
Chambersburg PA
CBHW040252100426
42811CB00011B/1230